Doorway to Christmas

Doorway to Christmas

Christmas Sentiments
Illustrated With Photos

Pedro Hernandez

The Hermit Kingdom Press
Cheltenham ♦ Seoul ♦ Bangalore ♦ Cebu

DOORWAY TO CHRISTMAS: CHRISTMAS SENTIMENTS ILLUSTRATED WITH PHOTOS

Copyright © 2005 by Pedro Hernandez

ISBN 1-59689-011-8

Write-To Address:

The Hermit Kingdom Press
3741 Walnut Street, Suite 407
Philadelphia, PA 19104
United States of America

Info@TheHermitKingdomPress.com

★ ★ ★ ★

Hermit Kingdom
12 South Bridge, Suite 370
Edinburgh, EH1 1DD
Scotland

http://www.TheHermitKingdomPress.com

For Charlie

"Which Christmas is the most
vivid to me? It's always the
next Christmas."

-- Joanne Woodward

Contents

Christmas Traditions <13>

"Doorway to Christmas" <20>

Gifts and Christmas <22>

"The Christmas Gift" <37>

Christmas Food <39>

"Christmas Party" <51>

Christmas with Relatives <54>

"Family Christmas" <65>

Christmas and Religion <67>

"Christ-child" <72>

"Immanuel" <74>

Christmas Aftermath <76>

"Next Christmas" <90>

Doorway to Christmas

Christmas Traditions

Christmas is a wonderful time of the year. It is a time for chestnuts roasting on the fire. Family traditions are brought up, and kids are reminded of the strange family Christmas traditions that supposedly connect them to the past and their dead ancestors.

Christmas is a kitchy holiday in many ways. And American consumerism plays up sentiments. It's a time to be giving, so crack out your American Express card! Santas on street corners are collecting for various charitable causes. And you get the strange feeling in your stomach that some of these Santas are collecting for their own greedy coffers.

Yet, Christmas is special. We want to keep believing in the

miracle of Christmas. Miracle on the 34th Street. It's a Wonderful Life. Christmas makes us want to believe. It makes us want to put faith in something that is greater than ourselves.

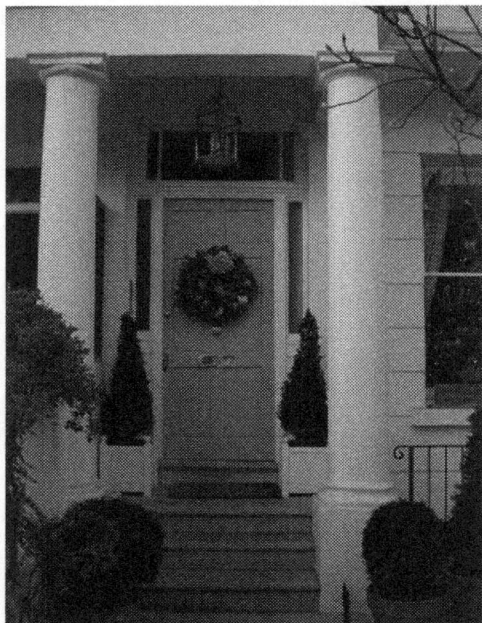

Christmas makes us want to believe that there is a doorway to our dreams and that all we have to do is knock on the door.

And the door will be opened to us.

It seems like even if all goes wrong every other time of the year, Christmas will always be different. Christmas is equated with the miracle of Christmas. Things will go right on Christmas. We hope and we believe.

And it is a kind of faith in the miracle of Christmas that keeps parents wanting their kids to believe in the miracle of Christmas. Family traditions are encouraged. Parents want their kids to believe in the magic of Christmas through practicing various traditions. Some want them to believe for all of them.

Christmas trees are raised. Some families keep a tradition of adding a special new ornament to the family Christmas tree each year. Some families make an effort to decorate rooftops with lots of lighting. Some families encourage their kids to leave milk and cookies for Santa. Some families make a habit of hanging up the same door wreath every year.

As dull as some Christmas ornaments may seem, they remind us of the magic of Christmas. They add to the fuzzy memories of Christmas for us. We remember kitchy Christmas traditions we had. And we want to pass on the memories of Christmas and fuzzy feelings of Christmas to our posterity.

Christmas is about traditions in many ways. Traditions we have inherited come alive in the festive season. We want to create traditions for our friends and loved ones. We want to be a channel of wonderful traditions that will add to the magical experience of Christmas.

I have personally started to collect a piece of nativity scene wherever I go. That way, at Christmas time, I can have a magnificent nativity scene for all to enjoy. It's like building a train network in your home. You might have seen an elaborate train set, some even occupying a whole room. That's what I want for my nativity scene. I just started this tradition, but I would like it to be a magnificent little town of Bethlehem, with nativity pieces from around the world. Who knows? Maybe it'll become a museum installation some day?

I think it's great to pass on fuzzy traditions and create new ones. And yes, I don't mind you sharing

my tradition of building an
awesome nativity scene.

Traditions make Christmas that
much more special. Traditions
make us connected to the past.
Traditions add to the magic of
Christmas.

"Doorway to Christmas"

It is like a road to heaven:
Doorway to Christmas
That is --

Full of hope and promise,
Wishes for the future,
Desires of the present.

Christmas wreathes
Adorn the door
With magic and sentiment.

Who cannot but believe
That with a knock or two
The door will be opened?

The magic of Christmas
Is adorned in the front door –
A doorway to Christmas.

Christmas awaits inside
With all the warmth
And kindred spirit.

Festive hearts are
Just behind the
Doorway to Christmas.

Gifts and Christmas

It's difficult to talk about Christmas without talking about Christmas gifts.

Santa Claus is a fuzzy dude who brings cool gifts.

You better watch out and you better not cry because Santa Claus is coming to town!

Christmas is about giving gifts to loved ones. It is one time of the year even the emotionally most inexpressive can send a sentimental Christmas card. It's a time when gushing mooshy-gooey feelings won't get you in trouble. You have a pass-jail card for even being more sentimental than the most tear-jerking of Christmas specials on TV.

Gift-giving has become an important part of celebrating

Christmas. Christmas gifts have become an important key to the doorway to Christmas and happiness-sharing that lies behind the door.

What kind of gifts is good for Christmas? This is a question that has been asked by millions of people in the past and the present. And it's the question that will be asked for many more years to come. I would like to help those who are completely clueless.

The rule of thumb for Christmas gift-giving is to go for the sentimental value.

Christmas is all about sentimentality. Traditions. Christmas programs. Christmas Trees. Ornaments. Christmas door wreaths. They are all meant to make you feel all gooey and goose-bumply for the festive season.

So, it's a good idea that your Christmas gift fits the atmosphere of the holiday.

Sentimental is definitely the way to go.

But sentimental is not always easy to do. It requires thought and care.

Sentimental gifts may not always be the most expensive, but they are the most difficult to buy because they require a lot of thought and reminiscence to capture the fuzzy-factor.

I will offer some suggestions as a way of help. My advice is meant to be general, so it may not fit your case particularly. You can nonetheless use my advice as a reference point in the least.

Let's start with dad. What should you get dad? Generally, it is a safe bet if you assume that your dad still looks at you as if you were still 7 years old. It's like the golden age for dads. The child is young enough that he is completely dependent on him. Dads generally like the feeling of being needed. The feeling of being a protector makes him feel good about himself. Christmas is the perfect time to reassure your dad of his feelings.

So, a good idea for dad's Christmas gift is to get him something that will fit his image of you as still his child. Get him a Christmas sweater with Rudolf the Red-nosed Reindeer on it. Get him a fluffy, yet somewhat macho stuffed animal, perhaps like Garfield. Such gifts reassure your dad that you think of him as if you were still his little boy.

You might think that buying a Christmas gift for mom is similar. But it's not really the case. Yes, it is true that moms generally look at their children with a mother-hen-like instinct. However, unlike the dads out there, moms generally are less

captivated by illusion. Moms
know that their children are
their children, but they don't see
them as 7 year old children.
Moms tend to be more realistic
about the children growing up.

What this means is that moms
generally expect a gift that have
a sentimental value and also a
financial value. In other words,

it's probably a good idea to cough up some dough for your mom. After all, she carried you in her womb for 8 months, you should be more than happy to splash a little for your dear o' mom. Right?

Generally, you can't go wrong with some type of jewellery item. A pendant, necklace, broach, ring, earrings, etc.

Clothing items can be good if you know her taste. If you don't know her taste, then, it's probably not a good idea to risk it this way. Moms generally tend to be much pickier about the clothing item they wear than dads.

But remember, whatever you buy, keep the value of sentiment in mind. So, for instance, if you are going to buy a broach, think about an item that will allow her to show off to her friends. For instance, buy a nice pendent with "best mom" written or it. If you want to be more subtle about it, you could have something sentimental like that engraved on it.

Buying for siblings is a bit easier. First of all, you can buy things that you would like since they are probably close to your age group. Getting them hip clothing would generally work. For sisters, novelty clothing items may make them smile. Give them something they can use for special occasions. Give them something that will remind them of you. They can always tell their friends, "See how wacky this item is? It's a Christmas gift from my brother!"

As a general rule, it is safe to assume that sisters do not look at brothers like they view other men. For most women, father and brothers are in the special category. So, even if "all men are pigs," father and brothers are not in that category. Because you are in the special category, you can be a bit more kitschy. What may seem like a stupid gift when given by other men, when a brother gives the kitschy gift, it may actually win a lot of brotherly points with sisters. It's what I call a special sibling bond.

In some ways, buying for brothers is easiest for males. Generally, men share a similar taste. Get them what you would like to receive and you would be on the safe side.

Now, we come to the really difficult part – shopping for your better half.

This is a tricky area because your girlfriend or wife will generally have expectations. You can't blame them because a part of them loving you is wanting you to love them. And generally women tend to bank a lot on the gift

that their lover gives them.
Women think that the gift
testifies to the sentiment of love.
In a sense, the Christmas gift
shows how much you love them.
It is like your love embodied.

It may seem a bit silly to blokes,
dudes, and hipsters out there,
but that's the way the cookie
crumbles. So, better accept the
reality and get something that
will not get you in deep waters.

First of all, remember that
Christmas is a sentimental
holiday, so your Christmas gift
has to be very, very sentimental.
In fact, it has to be far more
sentimental than the last gift
that you gave her.

A great sentimental Christmas
gift does not necessarily imply an
expensive gift. But a great
sentimental Christmas gift
requires a lot of thought and
care.

A great sentimental Christmas
gift will tie together wonderful
experiences you have shared in
the past with the present
Christmas season.

For instance, if you had your
first date in an Italian restaurant
named Don Giovanni's, you can
get tickets for Mozart's opera by
the same name. Include

something nice along with the two opera tickets. For instance, you can include nice earrings.

Let me give you another example of a good sentimental gift for your girlfriend or wife.

If she ever mentioned that she likes a certain animal – say, for instance, zebras – then you can get a little fluffy zebra that she can snuggle up to. Maybe you can include a sweater that has zebra patterns along with the gift. I guarantee you that she'll be tickled pink.

Of course, every lovey-dovey couple shares a different set of experiences by in large, so you'll have to do some thinking and get gifts that are sentimental in your case. But you get the drift from my examples. It's important to focus on the sentimental value of shared experiences.

The importance of focusing on the sentimental factor is true for a new couple as well as for those who have been married for over 50 years.

Christmas is a very romantic holiday. Keep the love alive!

"The Christmas Gift"

Peering up the chimney,
I wonder what Santa will bring
Me for Christmas.
I have been really, really good.

I put out milk and cookies
For Santa dearest
And hope to catch a glimpse
Of the hope of Christmas.

I stay awake and try
To stay in a watchful state
Because I want to see
The red symbol of happiness.

I feel my eyes close
In the fatigue of
All the running about
Celebrating the festivities.

What seems like a second
Passes by,
And I awake
And see something before me.

It's a gift
That Santa left me.
But the gift I wanted
Was to see my dear Santa.

Christmas Food

Let's face it. There is a lot of
eating at Christmas time. It's
almost as bad as on Thanksgiving.
In fact, it may be worse.
Whereas gluttony on
Thanksgiving is confined to a day,
massive food consumption at
Christmas time is, well, season-
long.

You can go to your office
Christmas party, and if your
place of work is of any worth,
there should be ample amount of
food – in fact, there should be
"too much" food.

You can go to several Christmas-
type soiree's of friends and
acquaintances that take before
the Christmas day itself. Food
generally never runs out at these
events. And if your friends are
Hispanic, you can guarantee that
there will be lots of food and

also the expectation that you will consume to your excess.

And then there is the Christmas Eve and the Christmas day meal itself. Food will be gushing out all over the place. If you have relatives fit for anything, you should be having nightmares about food after Christmas because you had so much of it.

To a large extent, Christmas and food become synonyms. I want to offer some advice to surviving the flood of food at Christmas time.

First of all, take slow bites. That way, it looks like you have a lot of food on your plate. People passing by you at parties will think that you are eating a lot. And do put on a smile, so that people will think you are enjoying your food. If you don't put on a smiley face, people may think that you are not enjoying your food, or worse, that you are not eating a lot. Covering up not eating in excess (as expected) will require a face that seems satisfied. Remember, you may have to go to several of these gluttony sessions, so pace yourself.

Second of all, talk a lot. Of course, conversation should be about little things – nothing too serious. After all, it's a Christmas party, ain't it? As long as you don't say anything damaging to yourself, it's a good idea to keep the small chat flowing. Talking gives you excuse not to eat too much (if that is your desire). Besides, you will come off looking like a very fun person. You'll stand out like a flash of light on a wooden door.

The third trick is to keep the food flowing to others. Phrases like – "Would you like more of that, Martha?" – keep you off food trouble. Spice up your comments with "Isn't that food just delightful?" Saying little things like that will take the focus off of you not eating and put attention on the food itself. This way, you will please the party-host and keep yourself from a senseless gluttony that may leave little space for the next big Christmas shindig.

Besides the advice on how to survive the Christmas food flood, I would like to offer some advice that I think will be very helpful to you. This is for those of you who plan to throw a Christmas party. Heck, I would say, go ahead and throw a Christmas bash if you haven't done so already. It's no good to be known just as a moocher, you know. Especially if you have a girlfriend or a wife, people will not think that you have an excuse not to take on the role of the Christmas party host.

And my advice will keep you at the head of the game. You will be known as the Christmas Party Host King. So, read carefully.

First of all, decorations are important. Even if the food is lousy, if the decorations are impeccable, you will have people impressed with the party.

Since it is Christmas, the best decorations should have lots of shiny stuff. I am being completely serious here. Get as many blinking lights as possible. If you think you have too much lighting, go out and buy a few more Christmas blinking-light sets. More the merrier! Trust me on this one.

If you want to be really fancy with a fun Christmas atmosphere, go for the White Christmas look. Buy some cotton balls, make some popcorn, buy some of the fancy snow-looking stuff from the nearby Christmas store, and decorate, decorate, decorate. If you think it looks like there is snow inside the living room, others will think so, too. Get second hand opinion. Call your best buddy over and ask him if it looks like Christmas inside your home. If you are going to the trouble of throwing a Christmas party, you should go way out. You don't want to be known as that lame-o who can't throw a Christmas party, do you?

Decorations are important, but food is too. But when I say food, I don't mean the quality of food. Sure, good quality food is important. But what's more important than quality is quantity. There is no Christmas party that is as bad as running out of food. Food must not run out. That is the Christmas party credo. Food, food, and more food.

Generally, Christmas parties tend to be large affairs. The way to survive that as a host is to have a lot of food that are side items. Have nachos with cheese and salsa dip. Have avocado. Have pizza slices in ample amounts. You can have fried chicken in bucket loads. Have enough of these side items that there will be basketfuls of crumbs left over like when Christ Almighty fed the five thousand.

To add a nice touch to all the
food, have one or two items that
are particularly special. You can
have a special ham from Norway
for instance. Or you can have a
sushi platter. It makes for an
aesthetic pleasure if not a
culinary one. And a bit of that
exotic factor can't hurt.

Besides the crazy decorations
and the surfeit of food, you
need something else without
which a Christmas party would
not be the same.

Of course, what I refer to is a
good dose of mushy Christmas

music. You heard me right. You need Christmas music. Non-stop!

Christmas party is not Christmas party without Christmas music. Tacky Christmas music. Funny Christmas music. Traditional Christmas music. You name it. If it has anything to do with Christmas, then you should add to your collection. You need hours and hours of Christmas music. If you could help it, have Christmas music blaring in every room of your house. Dang it, don't forget. It's a Christmas party.

Of course, you can add to the three essential advice points above. Whatever you add, whichever improvisations you make, you must have the above three essential ingredients.

If you follow my advice, you can be known as that cool Christmas Party Host. You may acquire a

new status in your
neighbourhood or in your
workplace. Go on, be a
Christmas Party Mega-Host.

Enjoy serving Christmas food.

And enjoy eating Christmas food.

Make Christmas food a part of
your joyful Christmas!

"Christmas Party"

I went to a Christmas party.
I knew not what to wear.
I knew not what to bring.
I knew not who would be there.

It was a Christmas party
With a company of strangers
Although important people.
I was scared, I guess.

I went to the Christmas party
Not knowing what to expect.
But I survived
And thrived.

Why?
How?
I just kept eating and eating.
And I became sick.

All the eating
Made me feel good at the time
But now
I am paying for it.

I guess I am not made
To eat and eat
And be okay.
Now I run like a mad nun.

And I don't know
When I will be well again.
You see,
I ate too much.

That Christmas party
Was my undoing.
I don't know
When I will be whole again.

Christmas with Relatives

Many Americans are scattered all over the map. It seems like many Americans leave the home of their parents when they go to college. Even if the college dorm is 30 minutes away from home, it seems like the beginning of a new life.

Once in college, it is never sure where you will end up. Job may take you out of the city and even away from your home state.

It almost seems like the American way to seek your dream and fortune by roving around. America was built by a bunch of itinerants after all, no?

During Christmas season, many Americans make the journey back home. Once a year, Americans fly back to their hometown to see parents, siblings, childhood friends, and relatives.

Once back home, there will be a lot of time spent with relatives. Many American families are in the habit of inviting extended family – aunts, uncles, grandparents, granduncles, nieces and nephews – for Christmas festivities.

Not surprisingly, some of the worst family feuds occur at Christmas time.

It could be a combination of "cuz, haven't seen you in ages" and "dude, don't look down on me because I am like thousand times smarter than you."

You get the drift. There can be a number of reasons why conflicts flare. Personalities clash. Bad memories from the past seem to crop up at the worst moments. And it doesn't help that your well-intentioned granny keeps reminding you all of all the troubles from the past. She may be going senile, but boy she can do so much damage!

Most families that open up Christmas celebration to extended family of relatives generally experience some kind of conflict.

How can you cope with all the craziness?

Here are some helpful suggestions which might save you during Christmas time.

First of all, figure out some diversion tactics. For instance, if you see conflicts flaring up between relatives over some petty memory from the past, try to provide the antidote to the poisoning of the social scene by providing some happy memories from the past.

But remember, bad memories tend to be more potent. So if a memory is pretty bad, then you have to come up with a memory that is not pretty good, but really, really good to counteract the malignant effects.

You must have an arsenal of happy memories ready. If a bad memory is thrown in like a grenade, you must jump on it and neutralize it before it explodes. If you do not have prepared happy memory accounts handy, you will probably not be quick enough to diffuse the situation.

Secondly, you must appoint someone as a back-up person. The person can be your wife or

your mother. You must find
someone who has a vested
interest in the success of a
smooth Christmas celebration.

If you fail to respond in time,
your partner can jump in and
help you. And you can play the
positive force off of each other
to diffuse the situation. We can

call this "tag-team-defuse-
method."

But having defensive mechanism
in place is not enough. You have
to have some offensively positive
mechanism in place. In other
words, pre-empt the negative
forces by flooding the room with
many happy memories of the past.
Remind the relatives of the joy
of Christmas. Remind the
relatives of the benefits of the
bond of being relatives. Remind
the relatives of all the good
things that they can benefit from
by not indulging in negative
energies.

Offensive positive strategy can
be helped by having momentos of
happy memories. Strategically
place photos of happy times.
Hang symbolic objects from
successful outings with relatives.
For instance, if the relatives in
question enjoyed a trip to the
zoo with you, then have a banner

from the zoo hanging prominently near the Christmas tree.
Strategic placement of happy memory objects will go a long way to making your relatives get along together in the convergence of many in the festive season called Christmas.

Another tactic to help smooth over gathering of relatives is to

have soothing, almost hypnotic Christmas carol playing in the background.
Find a cherubic soprano singing traditional Christmas songs. Test out the soothing factor before the gathering. Play the chosen CD and try to think about negative thoughts. If the CD seems to soothe you as you think about the negative memories, then it will probably work for your relatives as well.

Most importantly, the secret to surviving a Christmas filled with relatives is to convince yourself beyond the shadow of doubt that you want all your relatives there – down to the last 150th aunt.

Without girding yourself with a firm conviction that you want this gathering of relatives to happen, it will be difficult for you to hang onto your defenses.

Your sanity may be at stake, for goodness sakes!

So, be strong and first prepare yourself mentally and psychologically.

Erect a psychological fence against all that brings negative

thoughts flooding into your
mental system.

And open the door to positivity
and happy memories.

"Family Christmas"

I want to celebrate
A family Christmas
Including all the relatives,
All my blood-kin.

Flesh and blood
Am I
And I want to be with those
Who are linked to me

By nature's design.
Christmas is a happy season
That brings loved ones together.
Who better to love

Than those who are linked to me
By blood and flesh
And by nature's design?
So give me

A grand old
Family Christmas!
I want my family near me
On Christmas day.

I want to open gifts
With family by my side
And all my relatives as well.
They are my flesh and blood.

Christmas and Religion

Let us face it. Christmas is a
Christian holiday. In fact,
without Christianity, we would
not have Christmas.

Given that Christmas is a
Christian holiday, should there
be embarrassment celebrating
Christmas with all the holiday
trimmings of Christianity?

Being from a Catholic family
meant that Christmases were
very special.

Going to the midnight Christmas
mass with the family was not only
normal but a memorable thing to
do as a family.

Having a nice nativity scene in my
front yard seemed so natural.
And I am happy to have a great
nativity project of my own now
as an adult.

I am unabashedly happy to celebrate a very Christian Christmas.

There is no need to hide behind a bush. Christmas is a wonderful Christian celebration.

Christmas celebrates the birth of the Christ-child.

I like to sing Christmas carols. And let's face it. Most of the Christmas carols are about the Christ-child.

Why should I feel embarrassed about singing them? Why should I feel embarrassed about my religion?

I figure, Christmas is one time of the year that I can unashamedly celebrate my religion.

I know it may sound negative to emphasize the Christian element in Christmas. But let's be honest here. Christmas is a holiday founded on the idea of celebrating the birthday of the Christ-child.

So, to Hades be the PC culture!
Political Correctness should not
muzzle me from celebrating the
great Christian holiday of
Christmas.

So there! I have said it. And I
am proud!

"Christ-child"

On that First Christmas
When all were asleep
A star from the east descended
On the city of Bethlehem.

Wise men from the east came
To give honor and praise
To the Christ-child
Born to save.

Shepherds from the fields
Came to worship
The little, tiny babe
On a manger.

Angels on high
Sang and sang
And sang
Yet more.

Angels sang to honor
The Christ-child,
God who took on human flesh,
God-Incarnate is He.

Eternal light of God
Shone in the face
Of the Christ-child
Born as God-Man.

"Immanuel"

Immanuel,
You are God with us,
God who came in human form,
God-Man you are.

Immanuel,
Called Christ Jesus on earth,
You have taken on human flesh
In order to die for us.

Immanuel,
You are a true embodiment
Of love, peace, and hope,
For you are God.

Immanuel,
You have freed us
When you freed yourself
From the shackles of death.

Immanuel,
Power of Satan
Could not keep you
In the grave.

Immanuel,
Blessed be the day
You were born on this earth.
Joy to the world!

Christmas Aftermath

No consideration of celebration of Christmas will be complete without looking at what to do after Christmas. Sometimes, it's important to deal with the practicalities of the matter.

Let us first deal with the question of what to do with the Christmas tree.

I don't encourage just throwing Christmas tree away. It feels like the Christmas tree deserves a

special treatment than just being
thrown together with refuse.
Wouldn't you agree?

I have several suggestions for
what to do with the family
Christmas tree.

Suggestion number one: burn it.
No, I don't mean in a
disrespectful way. It's like
offering up incense to God with
the precious cedars of Lebanon.

If you have a fireplace, then the
burnt offering of the Christmas
tree is ideal. Your family can
enjoy the plenty of the Christmas

tree even further. There can be more smiles and laughter in front of the Christmas tree. Christmas tree will indeed provide you and your loved ones with further warmth of Christmas.

As you sit by your fireplace, you can share fond memories of the

Christmas just passed together. You can reminisce about all the good things that have transpired. More positive Christmas spirits will be bubbling over in your warm hearth.

To enjoy the Christmas spirit to the fullest extent, drink some hot chocolate with marshmallows floating on top. Bake some

marshmallows on top of the fire
as vestiges of the Christmas tree
are offered up in sweet aroma.

Another way to give further
Christmas life to your Christmas
tree after Christmas is to use
the wood and pines for an
artistic creation. You can create
a sculpture or a type of collage

work. This way, you encapsulate the beauty of this Christmas for years to come.

Hang up your artistic creation in the family room. Treasure the newly reincarnated Christmas tree in a nouveau object d'art in your personal room.

Your Christmas tree does not have to end up in a dingy dump site. It can give you more Christmas cheer.

Besides the Christmas tree, there are other things from

Christmas you will have to think about.

What are you going to do with all the lighting?

The practical solution is to put them into a box and store it in a safe place (certainly, a place that you will remember) until the next Christmas.

You could be a bit more creative than that.

If you have many rooms, you can decorate one of the rooms as a Christmas room. You can make the room into something like a Neverland that brings hope and happiness. Whenever you are depressed, you can just hop into this room and be cheered up.

But if you are like the most of us and do not have a spare room to decorate into a Christmas room, you don't have to fret. You can do something with the lights.

You can set up lighting in one corner of your room. You don't have to turn it on 24 hours per day. But when you feel a bit down, you can light up the Christmas lights and be immediately cheered up.

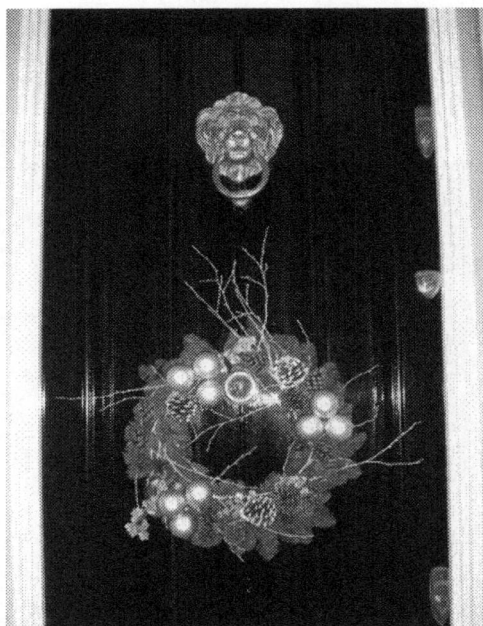

If you take some care, you can set up the Christmas lights in a way that they don't look too intrusive.

When the Christmas lights are not lit, the room will look normal, like any other room. But when the lights are turned on, voila! You have something very special.

Having something cool like this set up can make for romantic moments with your loved one.

Let your imagination run wild and let the artist in you shine!

And what are you going to do with your Christmas cards? I know some people who receive hundreds of Christmas cards every year. Often, there are some really incredible looking Christmas cards.

I remember a friend of mine who has been so blessed with numerous friends and admirers, and he made Christmas cards

into a type of a wall-paper for his
basement. It actually looked
very cool. There was something
to look at during dull moments
and jump-start conversations.

Even proper folk like that kind
of thing. It is wacky, zany, and a
bit artistic. It's like a collage of
your basement wall.

If you are ecologically conscious, you can recycle your Christmas cards.

How do you do this? You can cut out the front side of the card containing the picture as long as there are no words written on the back. And then you can cut out a hard piece of white paper roughly the size of the picture card. Then you can tape them together with an aesthetically pleasing tape or a transparent tape. If you can find a way to glue them on in a way that looks slick, go for it.

If you do a good enough job, it may look better than the original. You can be cutesy and write on the back of the new Christmas card creation, "Recycled by me for your Christmas pleasure." You can even include a short piece of paper describing ecological issues.

By next Christmas, you may
receive many accolades from
friends for being ecologically
friendly. You have recycled!

And everyone knows that it
takes more time to design your
card like that than just to buy
some from the store. So, your

friends may feel more special and you will win extra browny points.

Who says that all good deeds have to go punished? Not I. No sir-ee!

Après-Christmas can be fun, constructive, and memorable. It's up to you to make it so.

This world is a beautiful place, and you can make it even more beautiful with what you make of it.

It is up to you. It is all up to you.

Say to yourself, "I can do it! I can make après-Christmas a wonderful thing!"

The power of positive Christmas thinking! Sweet, ain't it?

"Next Christmas"

I am already thinking
About next Christmas.
For I know
That it will be better
Than the one just passed by.

Christmas is special
Every year.
Year after year
Happiness of Christmas
Adds to joy overflowing.

Next Christmas
Will add more joy
And happiness
In the basket of
Christmas memories.

I can't wait until
Next Christmas
Because I know
It will be very special.
Christmas is beautiful.

How wonderful it is
To be a part of the glory
That is Christmas!
With each passing year,
I partake of Christmas miracles.

About the Author

Pedro Hernandez is a lover of Christmas. He loves all things about Christmas, including all the hassles and headaches. This is his first book about Christmas, but he hopes that it won't be his last.